FIVE STAR
RAW SPA CUISINE
WITH CHEF BRYAN AU

*Sunflower Lord,
you're Super
Rawesome!!* ☺

RAW
☆
RAW ORGANIC
SAVING THE PLANET
RawOrganicSavingThePlanet.com

RAW
☆
RAW ORGANIC
SAVING THE PLANET
RawOrganicSavingThePlanet.com

RAW
☆
RAW ORGANIC
SAVING THE PLANET
RawOrganicSavingThePlanet.com

RAW
☆
RAW ORGANIC
SAVING THE PLANET
RawOrganicSavingThePlanet.com

RAW
☆
RAW ORGANIC
SAVING THE PLANET
RawOrganicSavingThePlanet.com

BRYAN AU

Five Star Raw Spa Cuisine With Chef Bryan Au
BY BRYAN AU
E-mail: RawBryan@hotmail.com

Website: www.rawinten.com

Bio & Intro Edited by Bryan Au
Art Direction & Design by Bryan Au
Photography by Bryan Au
Special Thanks to Cathy Jeffries

Copies of this book can be ordered from Amazon.com, Rawinten.com or through the author directly at:
RawBryan@hotmail.com

I would like to thank God, all of my family, friends and the Yoga and RAW Community for all of the love, support & adventures. Lets all bring more health, harmony, love, joy and peace to the World together forever and always!

INTRODUCTION

It is the healing loving intention of this book to present Raw Organic Cuisine as one of the most important and best new culinary cuisines in modern times. The reason is that it is totally new, unique and gourmet while being the ultimate in health food. Finally Chef Bryan Au has been able to blend the best in Raw Organic Cuisine into a new category that was inspired by 5 Star Spas and Resorts from around the World.

In the 1970's Raw Organic Food as it was called was mostly underground and enjoyed by "hippies", free thinkers and health seekers. In the 1980's pioneers such as David Wolfe emerged to promote a all natural way of eating, thinking and living. It quickly became a lifestyle and food trend well into the 1990's as more people discovered the all natural anti-aging effects, prevention of disease, reversal of many modern conditions such as cancer, diabetes, obesity but the most amazing aspect was the vibrant tastes and new flavors to be discovered and enjoyed in the RAW.

This trend quickly spread to Hollywood as more and more famous actors and actresses were reportedly also doing the "Raw Food" Diet as it was called. Actress Demi Moore did it for Charlie's Angels II and everyone marveled at how young, slim and amazing she looked especially compared with her much younger counterparts on screen. People were convinced and wanted to learn more. Then Super Model Carol Alt came out with her own 2 books about how RAW Food saved her life, health and improved her well being in two best selling RAW Books. Then the media reports Sting, Donna Karan, Academy Award Winner Forest Whitaker, Lisa Bonet, Alicia Silverstone, Woody Harrelson, Cher and many more start to reveal their RAW Food secrets and benefits to the World.

Meanwhile all this time Celebrity Raw Organic Chef Bryan Au was busy writing his RAW IN TEN MINUTES raw organic recipe book that rawcked the world with fast, fun and simple raw organic food that looked and tasted like everyone's junk food and comfort food favorites. It is still a best seller today and has expanded to Raw Organic Restaurants, Organic Ingredients & Snack Foodline, Eco Organic Fashions, DVDs, TV Shows, Media Appearances and much more. Now you are holding in your hands the latest creation FIVE STAR RAW ORGANIC SPA CUISINE WITH CHEF BRYAN AU. This book is a culmination of 12 + years of World travels, learning, experimenting and perfecting the new level of Raw Organic Food that is Raw Organic Spa Cuisine.

This new category is about making RAW Food ultra gourmet, light, rejuvenating and refreshing like any high end Spa experience should be. But emphasis is placed on gourmet presentation, super health benefits and gourmet flavor. Chef Bryan Au once again makes all of his techniques and recipes simple, easy, fast, fun and delicious! All of these recipes are still under 10 Minutes many of them even faster, fun and easier than in the previous 2 RAW IN TEN MINUTES books!

You will also find dishes that are inspired by more traditional spa cuisine like seafood, soups, sauces, the use of tropical fruits. But all the recipes in this book are 100% Vegan, Organic and RAW but they look and taste cooked, baked or deep fried. You will enjoy traditional spa cuisine like seafood as well as desserts.

You will find each recipe is deliciously easy, simple, fast and fun to make. Many people enjoy Spa Cuisine but it does not have to end when you go home, now you can enjoy 5 Star Raw Organic Cuisine as much as you want and you will find my recipes and techniques such a joy to prepare because it is now easy, simple, fun and amazingly delicious!

So lets have fun and enjoy the next level of health, well being, spa cuisine and in 5 STAR RAW ORGANIC SPA CUISINE WITH CHEF BRYAN AU.

TABLE OF CONTENTS

RAW

About Bryan Au

Bryan Au has quickly established himself as a premiere Raw Organic Celebrity Chef to the Stars in Hollywood and all around the World. He has worked with 5 Star Spas, resorts, chefs and restaurants and wanted to share all of his best new creations with everyone interested in fun, easy recipes that will give you vibrant energy and health. Many clients and people have come into his raw restaurant or asked him how to create lovely RAW Spa Cuisine in their home and this book was the answer. You will quickly discover that gourmet Raw Spa Cuisine is so simple, fast, fun yet fantastically delicious that you will want to share this incredible experience with everyone as well.

In this book there will be many recommendations and certain tools such as Ceramic Knives, Ceramic Peelers, Blendtec Blender, Excalibur Dehydrator, certain ingredients like Bryan Au's brand of Goji Berries, snacks, ingredients and more. These particular items are recommended for their price, value, performance, and very high standards. The Blendtec Blender is the BEST BLENDER in the World for example and ALL of the recipes in this book were created using the Blendtec. The reason why it is recommended is because of its perfect design and performance on top of value. Through Bryan Au's website you may purchase it for only $350 including tax, shipping and handling this is the best deal you can find anywhere and the Blendtec is so professional that it ensures a very high quality of blending and food every time. So please note that although yes you can use any brand, blender or kitchen equipment you like, the reason why certain ones are recommended in this book is because of the very high value, quality and performance that Bryan Au has thoroughly tested and only will use in all of his raw organic food preparations. Also the Blendtec Blender can do things that no other blender can and because of its superior design food does not hide or get stuck underneath the blades.

Next is the Ceramic Knives and Peelers which are HIGHLY recommended because Ceramic does not react with food like metal knives. What this means is added value and freshness to your food and organic ingredients. When you use and cut with Ceramic Knives the food will not brown or oxidize for a very long time. With any and all metal knives you can see your food browning and oxidizing very quickly. Not only that but Ceramic Knives do not require any sharpening for about 2 years, they do not rust, you won't get any metal ions or taste in your food and they are very easy to clean. Fact is Chef Bryan Au ONLY uses and recommends Ceramic Knives in all of his Raw Organic Food preparations and has his own high quality Signature series of Ceramic Knives and Peelers for your enjoyment and again at the BEST PRICES possible. Most Ceramic Knives cost around $100 to $200 each but Chef Bryan Au's RAW STAR signature series and brand is only around $20-$55 including shipping, handling and tax. Chef Bryan Au does this in order to allow everyone access to the best equipment, ingredients and more. There are also very high quality raw organic ingredients, Eco Clothing and more on the main website:

http://www.RawInTen.com

And for every purchase you make a new tree is planted and a certain amount of profits goes into various charities and humanitarian causes around the World so you are in fact part of the Global Family and are empowered to be Raw Organic Saving The Planet in the most fun, fashionable and delicious ways possible! Saving the World should be a celebration, fun and joyous so thank you for your support and I hope you will share all the new information in this book with your friends, family and loved ones.

I wish you all the best in health, wealth, love, joy and spirit,

Raw Organic Chef Bryan Au
http://www.RawInTen.com
http://www.RawOrganicSavingThePlanet.com

Equipment and Ingredients

This is the current Chef Bryan Au special signature series of Ceramic Knives! The Avocado on the right was cut with a conventional stainless steel knife and after 45 minutes is oxidizing and wilting, the Avocado on the left was cut with my Ceramic Knife and 45 minutes later is still pure, fresh and wholesome! I ONLY uses and recommends Ceramic Knives in all of his Raw Organic Food Preparations because they increase the value, freshness and taste in food. I only use a metal knife to open Coconuts and is the ONLY time I will use a metal knife. Ceramic Knives are very pure, light so you won't get fatigued, balanced, food won't brown or oxidize, you don't have to sharpen it for 2 years, and they are very sharp. I have BEST prices on these in the World so everyone can finally afford and have access to the best in everything! Most Ceramic Knives cost $100-$200 but my signature RAW STAR Signature Series is only around $20-$55 which includes shipping, tax and handling!

These are the new Ceramic Peelers with Chef Bryan Au's Signature and RAW STAR LOGO. The RAW STAR means that you are a all natural Super Hero and are in fact helping to protect your health, environment, community and the Planet in the most fun, fashionable and delicious ways possible! When you use the ceramic peeler your food stays fresh, won't oxidize or brown and it stays super sharp for many years to come. Get yours today on the website for only $7 including tax, shipping and handling. Most Ceramic Peelers are $15-$20.

The main reasons these products are recommended is because they add value to your organic food, preparations and are at the absolute best prices and quality possible. They also make food preparation more fun and easier to clean as well while literally being the BEST Products in the World.

Next is my personal favorite the Blendtec Blender!

I have used all different kinds of blenders in the World and the Blendtec Blender is the "Rolls Royce" of all blenders. The reason is the perfect blade and jug design on top of it being 3 horsepower with a digital computer chip that actually senses what you are blending and will control the speed and rpm to make each blend perfect. There are also soft push buttons, a lighted LCD Display and the blade will not hide your food or ingredients like most blenders. Cleaning is a snap and the Blendtec Blender will do things that no other blender can. Yes you can still use other blenders for my recipes but please note that I have created each and every recipe using the Blendtec so the measurements were designed with Blendtec in mind. Some blenders have huge or enormous jugs so you may have to increase the recipe's portions just to get it to blend. From my website you can order your Blendtec today for only $350 and this is the BEST price you can find anywhere, it is totally worth it because it will bring your Raw Organic Food preparations to the next professional high quality level. It is ALWAYS worth it to save and invest in high quality kitchen equipment, you will benefit from better safety, better food preparations, they last much longer so you don't have to keep replacing cheap blenders or equipment and they are always much easier to clean as well.

I also have a full line of very high quality Books, DVDs, Raw Organic Snacks, Ingredients, Eco Organic Bamboo Cotton clothing and much more so please check out my websites:

http://www.RawInTen.com
http://www.RawOrganicSavingThePlanet.com

And you can always e-mail me directly at:

rawbryan@hotmail.com for questions, consultations, classes, lectures, appearances or for sponsorships and business proposals.

Enjoy and thank you for joining the RAW Adventure and helping to save the Planet!

About the ingredients, I tried to only use and recommend easy to find ingredients that you should be able to locate at your local farmer's market, health food store or Whole Foods Market. If not then you can always buy directly from me and my website as well. Tibetan Goji Berries are new for a lot of people and they are so tasty, healthy and there are a lot of different ones to choose from but I have made sure that I have found the best quality, size and price possible on ALL of my products and ingredients. They all have my RAW STAR Logo and information on them and are available directly through my website but soon will be available in all the stores and markets nationwide!

I also highly recommend Miso Master's line of non-soy Chick Pea Miso. This has no soy in it so if you are interested in a no soy alternative with a delicious taste and source of protein then Miso Master is it. Some people still enjoy or like soy so you can use them in moderation with Miso Master or Cold Mountain as they make a very good affordable miso. South River Brand is very high quality and they make a Chickpea Miso by had but their prices are a bit higher. You can also try to experiment with my recipes by using lime, lemon or sea salt instead of any miso so please feel free to try different things and make my recipes more suited to your tastes. Sometimes when you play with the food or change something it can really improve it on many levels so have fun and try different things!

Again if you have any questions you can always e-mail me directly as I actually read and answer all of my e-mails, so it is like having your own personal Celebrity Raw Organic Chef at your fingertips:

rawbryan@hotmail.com

I hope you have a lot of fun with my recipes, products and please share with all of your family, friends, loved ones and the World!

Raw Organic Saving The Planet,
Bryan Au
http://www.RawInTen.com
http://www.RawOrganicSavingThePlanet.com

"Anchovy" Sushi, "Salmon" Sushi, Various "Sushi"

Everyone loves sushi and is one of the first things they think of when you mention raw food. But as we know there is a lot of mercury and pollution in our oceans and a serious decline of fish. But with Raw Organic Spa Cuisine you can still enjoy your favorite foods and recipes but in a more healthy and eco way! This is a good start and people LOVE this Vegan Gourmet "Sushi". We use Zucchini instead of seaweed because it is easier and more refreshing. Instead of using a Mandolin you should use my new Ceramic Peeler it is a lot easier and safer to use and you can peel the zucchini slices to make this delicious favorite recipe, enjoy!

About 10 Servings

2 Large Zucchini
Purple Cabbage Leafs
2 Avocados
Chick Pea Milo from Miso Master or South River Brand
Papaya and Pineapple from Hawaii
Soaked Sundried Tomato or fresh Roma Tomato
Sunflower Sprouts
Your Choice of favorite raw organic fruits and vegetables
Raw Star Brand Soaked Tibetan Goji Berries (Optional)

Using my Ceramic Peeler make long peelings from the zucchini and place on a plate like the photo to the right. Slice your favorite fruit and vegetables into small long pieces and place on one side of the zucchini slice like in the photo then start to roll it up and serve! The Papaya looks very similar to "Salmon" the soaked sundried tomato is similar to "Anchovy" and fresh tomato also is very similar to "Fish". You can also add my Tibetan Goji Berries that have been soaked in pure water for 20 minutes to make this a "super food" and to add more super nutrition to this recipe.

This is very easy and fun to make and many people will have "Sushi" rolling parties and everyone gets to make their own version then everyone shares and enjoys it together. In this recipe we add Chickpea Miso to get the salty flavor without having to use Nama Soyu or Soy Sauce so this is unique and different with less salt and more protein so give it a try. It is also a lot less messy too since all the ingredients are in the "Sushi" roll already. Try my Ceramic Peeler as the ingredients stays fresher longer and is much safer and easier to use than a mandolin.

"Stir Fried" Asparagus Tips with Pineapple Salsa

This is a really fun and easy raw organic recipe to make if you are in a hurry. It is very satisfying and people love it so give it a try! It serves about 3 people and it is best if you can find really small "baby" asparagus but it works with larger ones too. This recipe is very easy and just requires simple chopping, when you use my Ceramic Knives the food lasts so much longer and stays much fresher!

About 3 Servings

"Baby" Asparagus
Sundried Tomatoes in olive oil or soaked in water
Pineapple from Hawaii
Roma Tomato
Orange or Red Bell Pepper
Olive Oil
Dulse or Kelp Flakes and Cayenne Pepper Mixed
Sea Salt
Lime

Slice the Baby Asparagus into halves only using the tips and place on serving plate and drizzle with olive oil and sea salt and let marinate. Finely dice and sliver all the other ingredients in a bowl and mix well squeeze some lime on top and put on top of asparagus, sprinkle some Dulse or Kelp Flakes with Cayenne Pepper Mix on top and serve.

Pesto Zucchini or Eggplant

This is a super fast and easy raw organic recipe that should only take about 5 to 10 minutes to make. I have made this for people that are totally new to RAW Organic Cuisine and they were amazed at how refreshing and delicious it was. They really got more into Raw Foods after trying this recipe. Often times the most simple recipes can be the best too. You can use my Ceramic Peeler or a Mandolin for this recipe.

About 5 Servings

1 Yellow or Green Zucchini or Small Eggplant
2 Celery Stalks
Cayenne Pepper
Olive Oil
Chickpea Miso or White Mellow Miso
Basil
Pine Nuts
Sea Salt

If you use the Ceramic Peeler you can do your best to peel nice round shapes or cut the shapes you make with a knife into round circles or any shape you like. Otherwise use a Mandolin to make the thinnest slices of zucchini and celery possible. Place the final pieces on a serving plate like in the photograph. Put the last 5 ingredients into the Blendtec Blender and blend until very smooth. Then drizzle the mixture on top of the sliced celery and zucchini and sprinkle some cayenne pepper on top. Serve and enjoy!

"Crab" Sandwich and "Fried" Wonton with Crab

This is a very fun raw organic recipe that is keeping in the "Seafood" Dominated Spa Cuisine that is being served around the World. But we are 100% Raw Organic Vegan in this recipe book so part of the fun is coming up with the Raw Organic Version of classic or traditional foods. In this recipe finely sliced and chopped Radish mixed in either living hummus or brazil nut cheese becomes the "Crab". As you can see it looks very much like "Crab" and I similar but not exactly the same in taste but if you play with the recipe you can get it to become very close! Just add your favorite veggies, toppings and fixings. In the photo I used Mustard Greens as the "bread" but you can easily use lettuce, chard, red swiss chard or your favorite leafy green. And you can have many different sandwiches to enjoy!

About 4 Servings

Radishes
Cherry Tomato
Your favorite green leafy vegetable like chard, lettuce, etc. cut into triangle
Sandwich shapes
Pickles
Yellow or Orange Bell Peppers
Sprouts (I used Green Mung Bean Sprouts for a gourmet touch in the photo)
Avocado
Lime
Sea Salt
Living Hummus Recipe or Brazil Nut Cheese Recipe

Cut your favorite green leafy vegetable in small triangle sandwich like shapes then spoon in the "Crab" mixture and the rest of the ingredients to form a Sandwich. The "Crab" Mixture can be made in 2 different ways, with finely chopped radish mixed with either Living Hummus or with Brazil Nut Cheese to give it a creamy "Crab" consistency. To add more "Seafood" Flavor use kelp with cayenne pepper and lime on top with a little sea salt.

LIVING HUMMUS

Chickpea Sprouted
Tahini
Sea Salt
Olive Oil

Brazil Nut or Pine Nut Cheese

¼ Water
Olive Oil
Brazil Nut
Chickpea Miso (If you don't want to use miso you can try lime or lemon juice instead).

Blend until very smooth!

Photo of "Fried" Wonton with "Crab" you can also drizzle with Agave/Basil/Olive Oil/Miso blended together to give it a "Pesto" sauce, if you have fresh horseradish you can blend that in to make it zesty!

Fruity Tuna Wraps

This is a favorite at many spas around the World. Everyone loves "Tuna" fish with mayo because it is so creamy and a comfort food. Unfortunately our oceans are pretty polluted and Mercury occurs naturally in the ocean as well as being polluted by man. But we can still enjoy the creamy flavors and tastes thanks to my unique Vegan Tuna Fish Recipe, it is even creamier than any other version and is actually more healthy for you too. It does not come from a can and has the high quality protein, fats and benefits that your body loves so enjoy!

About 5 Servings

Napa Cabbage, but you can use Purple Cabbage, Lettuce, any greens you like…
Grapes
1 ½ Cup Cauliflower Tops
½ Walnuts
½ Lemon Juiced or Lime
¼ Cup Water
2 Tablespoons of Chickpea Miso
Sea Salt to taste
Dash Kelp Granules with Cayenne Pepper
Some olive oil to taste
Pickles

Peel about 5 leafs from the Napa Cabbage or Greens of your choice and set on a plate. Cut a few grapes in half. Blend the rest of the ingredients, except for the pickles, in the Blendtec Blender until smooth yet still chunky consistency. Spoon the "Tuna" mixture onto the Napa Cabbage leafs and chop some pickles and put on top, you can add red bell peppers for color too, enjoy! You will be surprised how creamy and "Tuna Fish" like this recipe is, it is refreshing, vegan with no mercury or toxins at all aren't you glad you discovered Raw Organic Cuisine?

18

Stuffed Zucchini Flowers with Pineapple Salsa, Chili Oil

I love sharing this very elegant example of what Raw Spa Cuisine is about, simple, refreshing, delicate and fantasy food that refreshes your soul and spirit. You have to get the zucchini flowers in season and you can also easily grow your own too! With the chili oil and chili pistachio nuts this takes on a gourmet experience.

About 4 Servings

4 Zucchini Flowers
Pineapple
Roma Tomato
Mango (optional)
Lime
Cayenne Pepper
Olive Oil
Sea Salt
Pistachio Nuts
Agave

Make sure the zucchini flowers are clean and place on a plate. Chop and Dice the next 3 ingredients and place in a bowl and squeeze lime over it and sprinkle some sea salt to taste, mix with a fork then gently insert the salsa into each zucchini flower. In a separate bowl mix cayenne pepper with olive oil and drizzle on top of zucchini flowers. Finally in a small bowl mix agave, cayenne pepper with pistachios and place on plate and serve. Do not eat the stems and only the flower part!

20

21

Avocado and Grapefruit Salad with Pickled Radish

This is a twist on a very popular and classic spa dish. The Acidity of the grapefruit compliments the creamy avocado while the new easy pickled radish recipe gives it a fresh bold 5 Star Raw Spa flavor!

About 2 Servings

1 Avocado
1 Radish
1 Grapefruit
½ Cup Apple Cider Vinegar
2 to 3 tablespoons of Real Raw Agave to taste
A green leafy garnish of your choice (dandelion is in the photo)
Yellow round mini zucchini (optional)

Prepare the avocado and plant the seed(to grow avocado tree!), peel and skin the grapefruit and cut into slices. With ½ of the avocado cut that in half and place on edge to form a circle like in the photo in the center of your plate. Then add the grapefruit also to form a circle on top of the avocado. Using the ceramic peeler or a ceramic mandolin or ceramic knife carefully cut the most thin slices of radish and yellow zucchini(optional). Also with the thin slices of radish cut very thin "noodles" or "toothpicks" and put into a bowl that is already mixed with ½ cup of Apple Cider Vinegar and agave. Let this sit for a few minutes to "pickle" the radish. Then after a few minutes put the thinly sliced radish on top of the grapefruit and also arrange the other slices around the plate to decorate it or put on top of thinly sliced yellow zucchini like in the photo. Put your favorite green leaf in the very middle as garnish and serve.

23

Samosas and Mini-Burgers

I often attend Hollywood Celebrity Red Carpet Events, Movie Premieres or Charity Events and I like to see what the Chefs are serving or creating. The cute smaller portions and snack inspired fun behind their recipes made me want to include it in my book. Recently I noticed they serve a lot of seafood and mini-burgers which are tiny versions of hamburgers. I immediately thought of a Raw Organic Vegan Version and my Samosa Recipe came to mind since you can now easily make either recipe because they are very similar and delicious.

About 5 Servings

Golden Flax Seeds
½ Cup Sunflower Seeds
Turmeric
Pickles
Roma Tomato
Pineapple
Mango
Olive Tapenade
Olive Oil
1/3 Cup Chick Pea Miso
¼ Cup Water
Curry Powder to taste

Blend the flax seeds in a Blendtec Blender I recommend this a lot because it will process the seeds in the best way possible, quickly and professionally. I don't even own a food processor because my Blendtec does it all! Blend until the seeds becomes a powder and pour into a large mixing bowl, add the miso, water, olive oil and mix with a fork and hands until well coated. Then roll into small balls and set aside. Chop up the other ingredients into tiny bite sized pieces except for the Olive Tapenade and Sunflower Seeds. In the Blendtec Blender blend and powder the sunflower seeds and pour into a mixing bowl, add the Olive Tapenade and drizzle some olive oil then mix with fork and hands until well coated this becomes the "ground beef" you can form mini "Patties" which becomes the mini burger. Put pickles, pineapple, mango and raw ketchup which is 3 to 4 pieces of soaked sundried tomatoes, fresh tomatoes, olive oil, ¼ cup water, a little apple cider vinegar all blended until smooth. And cut a flax ball in half and use as the "bun".

To make the samosas do not make the "burger" and you have samosas or add your favorite toppings some curry powder too.

Supreme Teriyaki "Rice"

This is a fun Asian inspired Raw Organic Cuisine Dish. The "Rice" is actually made of daikon and this can be served on its own or paired with other Entrees. The mint and pomegranate gives this recipe a very festive color and appeal. You can make this by hand or use a food processor if you are in a hurry of course we like to recommend the Off-The-Grid Eco Green Cuisine method of using your hands as often as possible!

About 3 Servings

White Daikon
Mint
Pomegranate
Agave
Dates
Cayenne Pepper
Cinnamon
Pistachio Nuts

Finely grate the Daikon by hand then chop it finely until a nice "rice" size. Then put in strainer and push down until all the juice and liquid is out of the daikon then in a small bowl put your mint and pomegranate in then place the chopped daikon in and press firmly so it all stays together because you are about to flip the bowl over so it has a nice round mound to it on a plate. Instead of hand grating and chopping finely you can also use a food processor with a grate blade then put it in with a S blade then put in strainer and follow through with the rest of the steps.

In the Blendtec Blender pour ¼ cup of agave and add 1 to 2 pitted dates and blend, this is the "Teriyaki Sauce" to be drizzled on top. And sprinkle some cinnamon and cayenne pepper too.

You can also use the "rice" in this recipe in your vegan sushi rolls, I also added the "cayenne, agave, pistachio" combo in this recipe which is mixing those 3 ingredients in a small bowl and adding it to the dish for crunch and flavor.

26

"Salmon" with Chili Oil & Mashed Potatoes

This recipe is so much fun because it looks so much like "Salmon" which is a very popular Spa type of entrée. But this version is vegan, raw and organic without all the mercury or toxins found in fish. And it is a fun twist on a traditional spa dish. In this recipe we use the Ceramic Peeler to make ultra thin slices of Organic Papaya. When we spice it with kelp and cayenne pepper, sea salt, olive oil or chili oil and squeeze some lemon on top it really takes on a salmon flavor. The "mashed potato" is actually not made of potato at all but is mostly cauliflower and nuts, this is so creamy and satisfying! There is even a "gravy" recipe to go along with it, enjoy!

About 3 to 4 servings

1 Large Papaya
Cauliflower
1 cup Walnuts
1/3 cup olive oil
Lime, dill and tomato for garnish

Thinly slice papaya and place on plate, squeeze lime and sprinkle salt on top, for a more "fishy flavor" sprinkle a combo of dulse and cayenne pepper on top(optional).

For mashed potato:

2 Cups Pine Nuts

1 Cup Cauliflower Tops

Finely chopped Rosemary

¼ Cup Olive Oil

¼ Cup Water

Dash of Sea Salt

3 Tablespoons Hawaiian Mellow White Miso

Pour the water into the Blend-Tec blender then add all of the above and blend until smooth. Garnish with dill.

27

"Bacon and Eggs"

This is a really fun World's First Vegan Raw Organic "Bacon and Eggs" recipe! Another Chef Bryan Au creation for your enjoyment. It is really fun because it is so easy and it really looks like fried "Bacon and Eggs!" there are not that many new Vegan Raw Organic Breakfast recipes out there, which is probably why my original Raw Organic Pancake recipe was stolen by other raw authors and chefs in their book, so in response I keep inventing new and original ones and you saw it here first folks! I am also inventing more raw organic recipes that have no nuts and no dehydrating(I am writing a special dehydrating book now). The "Bacon" recipe literally looks and tastes like deep fried bacon, the "Egg" is somewhat sweet but will help lower your cholesterol instead of increasing it! Enjoy!

About 2 Servings

1 Coconut
1 Papaya
Some dulse
Olive oil to taste

Carefully open up a coconut and carefully scrape out the inside "meat" so that it comes out in one whole piece if possible, this will take practice! After that using a ceramic knife cut some oval "fried egg like shapes and carefully place on your plate. Cut open the Papaya and carefully scoop out 2 round dome "Yolks" most likely you will get 2 that are really large so you will have to thinly slice them to make them "flatter and more yolk looking" then use a ceramic knife to cut them into more dome "yolk" shapes and place on top of the "egg" which is the young coconut "meat" on the plate. In another plate get some long shaped dulse pieces and marinate lightly in olive oil for a few minutes this will make it hard and crunchy like "bacon" and serve next to your "fried egg" enjoy!

30

Eggplant Manicotti with Tomato Sauce

We all LOVE Italian Food and Eggplant is not used a lot in Raw Organic Cuisine but it is one of my favorite vegetables so I had to come up with something amazing and delicious with it. I came up with this totally unique signature new creation, enjoy!

Servings 4

1 Thin (not round) Eggplant you want it to be ripe, semi firm
5 to 6 Tablespoons of Olive Oil
Kelp Cayenne Pepper
Sea Salt
1 Tomato
5 Pieces of Sundried Tomato (optional)
1 Red Bell Pepper
2 to 3 Olives
2 to 3 tablespoons of Miso Master Chickpea Miso
Basil or Parsley for garnish

Using my Ceramic Peeler carefully make very thin slices from the of the eggplant. Set aside 4 slices on a plate, thinly coat each side with olive oil and let sit for a minute. Then on each slice of eggplant put sliced olives and diced tomatoes down the middle to form a line. Next put in the Blendtec Blender red bell pepper, tomato cubed, sundried tomato that has been soaked in water for 10 minutes, olive oil, miso, Olive(optional for stronger flavor) blend until smooth. Spoon small mixture on one end of the marinated eggplant and roll up carefully and spoon more sauce on top, garnish with herbs and cubed red bell peppers and drizzle more olive oil.

If you want to add nuts to this recipe you can make a quick Alfredo Sauce for the inside and top: 1 Cup Pine Nuts, 2 Tablespoons Chickpea Miso, ¼ Cup Water, 4 Tablespoons Olive Oil, blend until smooth and use as "Cheese" or "Alfredo Sauce" inside and on top!

31

32

Pad Thai

This recipe demonstrates how Raw Organic Food can easily look and taste cooked. This is one of my popular recipes and people just can't seem to get enough of this one. It lasts for several days in the refrigerator if you do not put the sauce on top and it can be made a head of time. It is a good one to have on hand to share with guests.

5 Servings

2 Large Yams
2 Large Zucchini, one yellow and one green if possible
1 Cup Mung Bean Sprouts
2 Pieces of Kale
2 Purple Cabbage Leaves
Thinly Sliced Coconut Flesh
Bunch of Basil & Rosemary
1 Lime juiced
Kelp Granules with Cayenne
Olive Oil
¼ Cup Pine Nuts
Raw Organic Almond Butter

Using the Ceramic Peeler, make thin slices of yam and zucchini. Then using my Ceramic Knife, carefully cut length wise into long thin "noodles". Also cut the kale and purple cabbage leaves in the same way. Add the mung beans and mix all of the above in a large bowl and set aside. In a separate bowl mix the olive oil, dulse & cayenne pepper, juice from 1 lime all together then pour on top of the "noodles" mix. Then mix and serve with chopped: pine nuts, basil and rosemary on top. This is a very exotic colorful dish. You can add some fresh chilis to make it spicy!. M ix Almond Butter with lime juice and agave to make a more traditional Thai Sauce.

Tostada

I went to a friend's Raw Potluck Party and was reintroduced to the joys of beets! They are very delicious and refreshing raw with tons of antioxidants making this quick and easy "Tostada" a perfect Spa Cuisine recipe and addition. Also many people ask me for new raw organic recipes that does not have any nuts or dehydrating(new book coming out soon!) so this is one of those, enjoy!

4 to 5 Servings

1 Beet can use purple or golden
1 Carrot
1 Red Bell Pepper
1 Green String Bean
Olive Oil and Sea Salt (optional)

Simply slice the beets into thin slices and place on a plate. Slice the green string bean into slivers and add on top of the beets. Using the ceramic peeler make think shavings and add on top of the beets. Chop up the red bell pepper into tiny cubes and sprinkle on top. This is meant as a fast, simple quick and easy dish that is sure to please. You can also drizzle some olive oil and dash of sea salt on top but is really not necessary and is optional. The carrots looks like the cheese while the bell peppers looks like tomato. You can also add salsa, guacamole and other favorite toppings of course but sometimes simple and basic is the best too!

Pesto Kelp Noodles with Asparagus Tips

Kelp Noodles is all the rage in the Raw Organic Cuisine World at the moment because it is so quick and easy to use, you literally just have to open the package and rinse it. In this recipe with the Pesto Sauce and Asparagus Tips, it is a very high end spa gourmet meal also in an instant. In the photograph raspberries and basil is used as a colorful garnish but you can also use red cherry tomatoes cut in half as well.

About 3 Servings

1 Package of Kelp Noodles
1 Bunch of Asparagus
6 Fresh Basil Leafs
1/2 Cup Pine Nuts (no nuts is optional)
1/2 Cup Olive Oil
Sea Salt to taste (optional)
Raspberries as garnish (optional)

Open the Kelp Noodles package and rinse in pure water. Put into a mixing bowl. Cut the asparagus into tips and also into medium sizes set aside in bowl. In the Blendtec Blender add the Basil leafs, Pine Nuts (optional you don't have to use any nuts in this recipe), Olive Oil and blend until the Basil is very small like sand sized. Pour the Pesto over the Kelp Noodles in the bowl add sea salt to taste (optional) mix well and put on a serving plate, arrange with extra Asparagus tips on top and around as garnish (you may add the asparagus tips while mixing in the Pesto Sauce if you want it coated). You may want to marinate the asparagus in olive oil or cut into sliver and marinate to give them a more "cooked" taste and presentation (optional).
Serve and enjoy!

Japanese Style "Rawmen" Noodles

When in Tokyo, Japan please visit Veggie Paradise
which is the 1ˢᵗ Raw Organic Restaurant in Tokyo
and is owned by my friend Yuki Itoh!
I hope you enjoy this new creation of mine!
I use a new Kombucha technique that
will give the raw noodles an amazing "cooked" taste and add more
beneficial enzymes and probiotics to your good health!

1 to 2 servings

1 Butternut Squash (Yams to substitute if squash is not available)
1 Young Coconut
1 Persimmon (Mango or Papaya to substitute)
1 Radish
1 Bottle of Kombucha
Fresh Basil and Chives for garnish
Red Spicy Peppers and Seaweed for garnish (optional)

Using my signature series ceramic peeler "shave" the butternut squash
and put on a wooden or bamboo cutting board (never use plastic
butting boards the plastic will get into your food!). I suggest using my
signature series 8" Ceramic Knife for this recipe for the best precision
cuts to make the very fine and thin "rawmen noodles". You can't use
a spiralizer because it won't make the noodles as thin or fine as if you
do it by hand, I know it is a lot of work and tedious but if you have a
better way of making ultra thin fine noodles then use the 8" Ceramic
Knife and starting slicing the shaved peelings into the most fine
"noodles" you can, it will take about ½ hour to make each bowl and
serving of "rawmen noodles". Pour a bottle of Kombucha into a
serving bowl and put your sliced noodles in there. Allow to marinate
and soak as long as possible, best if you can cover and allow to soak
in the fridge overnight the next day it will have a "cooked"
consistency! Open a young coconut and carve out the "meat" into a
boiled egg shape. Do the same with the persimmon for the "yolk" top
with garnish and serve.

Coconut Thai Soup

This is a really good favorite all time raw organic soup recipe it is in this book because many exotic 5 Star Spas and Resorts are located in Thailand and many of them already serve raw organic cuisine. In this version we serve it in the coconut as a fun new way of presenting it but it is very hard to find and open coconuts so I suggest that you please use a serving bowl which is much easier and safer. I only used the fresh raw coconut in the photo for fun.

2 Servings

1 Fresh Young Coconut with the water & scraped coconut flesh
Some grated carrots, zucchini and small pieces of purple cabbage
1 Lime juiced
1 Teaspoon grated or chopped Ginger
3 to 4 Tablespoons of Miso Master Chick Pea Miso
¼ Cup Olive Oil
3 Cups Water
Finely Chopped Basil, Cilantro and Rosemary to taste
Kelp Granules with Cayenne to taste
Sea Salt to taste
½ Hot Chili Pepper for extra spicy flavor (optional)

Put all the above ingredients into the Blendtec Blender and blend until smooth and serve in a serving bowl, in the photo I opened up a young fresh coconut but this is dangerous and difficult to do so please do not attempt it is for presentation and photo purposed only! Garnish with lime, mung bean sprouts, herbs and spices!

Honey Dew and Cucumber Soup

This is a sweet dessert soup that is best chilled or used to keep you cool. The combination of Honey Dew and Cucumber is super refreshing and delightful!

3 to 4 Servings

1 Honey Dew Melon
1 Cucumber
3 Cups of Pure Water
Real Raw Agave to taste (optional)
Mint Garnish

Add the Water into the Blendtec Blender first then cut the Honey Dew Melon and scoop out the seeds and then scoop out the Melon and put into the Blendtec Blender, peel the cucumber with the Ceramic Peeler and chop into small pieces and put into the Blendtec Blender and blend until desired consistency, I suggest a slightly chunky one.

Drizzle with Real Raw Agave (optional since it is really sweet already) and garnish with mint. For a Variation and to give it more of a tangy flavor try adding some slices of Kiwi into the soup before blending this gives it slightly tangy interesting taste!

Pho

Using Chick Pea miso as the soup base and a variety of your favorite vegetables makes a Vegan Raw Organic Pho come to life! You can also use kelp noodles for fun too but just the veggies and hot peppers works really great in this traditional favorite.

About 2 to Servings

1 Purple Cabbage
1 White Cabbage
1 Napa Cabbage
1 Carrots
1 Cup Bean Sprouts
Some Grated Ginger
1 Lime
Miso Master Organic Chick Pea Miso

You may want to heat up some water to 114' or serve at room temperature this tastes best when warmed up and add the hot water into a serving bowl and mix with a few tablespoons of Chick Pea Miso to taste or desired flavor. Slice all the first 3 cabbages into very fine thin "noodles" using the 8" Ceramic Knife. This keeps it from wilting and keeps it fresher longer. Use the Ceramic Peeler to "shave" or "peel" the carrots into thin noodle shapes and add all the ingredients into the serving bowl with the Chick Pea Miso already mixed in. Add the sprouts, grated ginger, squeeze some lime and serve!

Spicy Chilled Peach Soup

This is a very traditional Spa type of soup but it is usually cooked with cream, there goes all the nutrition, vitamins, minerals and enzymes! With this version it is finally all natural, creamy, wonderfully RAWlicious! With all the benefits still in the soup so you can get that "glow" that everyone talks about. And the flavor...WOW! There are different versions and variations for you to try.

2 to 3 servings

2 Peaches
1 Cup Pure Water
2 Tablespoons Real Raw Agave (optional)
Cinnamon to taste
Hot Peppers to taste
Almond Milk (optional)
Mint and soaked Goji Berries for garnish (optional)

Peel and pit the 2 peaches then put all the ingredients into the Blendtec Blender and blend until smooth and serve! For Almond Milk put 2 cups of raw organic almonds into Blendtec Blender with 4 cups water and blend until really smooth and sieve through a nut bag or cheesecloth to get the Almond Milk and stir into Peach Soup!

To make the heart shapes on top put 2 "dots" of Almond Milk side by side next to each other then using a fork or chopstick poke through the hole and "drag" it towards the middle to make half of the heart and repeat with the other "dot". Serve chilled or at room temperature.

Dandelion and Kale Salad

Dandelion is a somewhat bitter green but is very healthy, detoxifying and it can help to rejuvenate your liver and kidneys. Most of us have had alcohol or other things that have taxed our kidneys and liver but raw organic dandelion has a ability to rejuvenate and strengthen them. Our kidney and liver's function is to filter out all the toxins in our blood so it is a very vital and important organ. In Traditional Chinese Medicine they often concentrate on rejuvenating the kidney and liver for this very reason but it happens to make a great salad and is great in smoothies too if prepared in the right way! I also enjoy Kale because it is a leafy green that is full of calcium, anti-oxidants and great benefits that is very refreshing in this delightful salad! This is showing up on more 5 Star Spas and Resorts around the World.

About 2 to 3 Servings

1 Bunch of Raw Organic Dandelion
1 Bunch of Dino Kale
Kelp and Cayenne Pepper
Olive Oil
Sea Salt
Lime
Raspberries and Figs (optional)

Cut and arrange the Dandelion (bought from a health food store) in a star or flower pattern on a plate. Chop up the Kale into bite sized pieces and arrange on top of the Dandelion. Drizzle olive oil on top of the salad and sprinkle the Kelp and Cayenne Pepper mix, sprinkle some Sea Salt to taste and squeeze the lime on top. Add the chopped figs (optional) and add the raspberries (optional). Some of your favorite sprouts, tomatoes, olives and favorite salad goodies can top of this light and refreshing new salad dish!

Donuts

This is a amazing new Donut recipe that does not have any nuts or dehydrating! Many raw recipes have nuts and people have asked me for no-nut recipes so they can keep slim, trim and their fat intake down to a minimum or to have raw organic recipes to enjoy that does not have any nuts, dehydrating and that is fast to make well here it is and in the form of a Donut!

About 3 to 4 Servings

2 Large Bananas
½ Cup of Golden Flax Seeds
Real Raw Agave

For Glazed Donut use Coconut Oil
Agave

For Chocolate Donut it is Raw Organic Carob Powder
Agave
Some water

For Cinnamon Donut just sprinkle Cinnamon on top of
Thin layer of Agave (optional)

Peel the 2 large bananas and put both in a large mixing bowl. Using a fork slowly mash the bananas then in the Blendtec Blender pour in the Flax Seeds and blend until a very fine powder then pour this into the bowl with the bananas and mix until evenly coated, adjust the amount of Flax Seeds to desired moistness and firmness of the Donuts, remember as the Flax Seeds gets absorbed into the bananas it will get harder and firm up and depending on the size of the bananas used which will vary, please adjust accordingly.

After the mixture is well mixed by hand form balls and poke a hole in the middle and flatten with your hand to form Donut shapes and place on a plate. For the Glazed Donut drizzle some Real Raw Agave (optional) and then lightly coat with Coconut Oil, you may drizzle a little more agave (optional).

For the Chocolate Donut mix some Carob Powder with Real Raw Agave to make "Chocolate Sauce" then add a little water to make it "glossy" and lighter then coat the donut with this. For a thicker chocolate sauce do not use extra water.

For Cinnamon Donut lightly drizzle with Real Raw Agave then sprinkle Cinnamon on top and serve! This is a totally new fun, fast and healthy Donut!

Cupcakes

We use the same "Donut" dough from the previous page as we do for the Cupcakes, what can be easier or healthier? Flax is very healthy especially when blended into a powder form it is easily digestible. Bananas are too but do use moderation and don't eat too many! If you cannot find flax or don't want to blend it yourself there is a very good company that makes Flax seed that are sprouted then made into powder form already called http://puravidaproducts.com I actually used their flax product in the photos they say that their product is sprouted flax and the amino acids absorbs better with their products and the shelf life is much longer. I really like their Flax it comes sprouted and already perfectly powered so less mess and cleaning with tons of benefits! I highly recommend them and will have their info and photo in the back of the book under the Ingredients Section!

About 3 to 4 Servings

Use the Donut recipe in the previous page but put it in fancy gold or paper cupcake cups. Then put your favorite toppings on top like Real Raw Agave (optional the dough is already sweet), Carob Agave "Chocolate Sauce" also from the Donut Recipe page. Or just add coconut oil for "frosting" (in hot areas it might melt so you may want to fridge the coconut oil first) and fruit and serve! The "sprinkles" are chopped Pistachio Nuts and Goji Berries!

52

Deconstructed Rootbeer Float

I have to admit I used to love to drink sodas and rootbeer was my favorite, but looking back now I wish I never touched a soda or drank them because they are so toxic and bad for you. But once again RAW saves the day with a low glycemic sweetener made of Real Raw Agave, some Rooibus Tea and Soda Water you now have a Raw Organic Rootbeer! I saw this item on the menu of a fancy resort and I immediately thought of a Raw Organic Version that is a lot of fun to make and to eat of course!

About 2 Servings

Almond Milk:
2 Cups of Almonds
3 ½ Cups of Water
4 Tablespoons of Agave
Vanilla Bean
Cinnamon
Agave
Rooibus Tea
Soda Water
Mint and your favorite fresh seasonal Berries for garnish

Make Vanilla Raw Organic Ice Cream by making Almond Milk which is 2 Cups of Almonds and 3 ½ Cups of pure Water in the Blendtec Blender and blend until very smooth, then sieve with nut bag or cheesecloth. Save the almond milk and pour back into the Blendtec Blender and then sprinkle a little tiny bit of cinnamon and cut the Vanilla Bean and scrape all the Vanilla in it and add to mixture in the Blendtec Blender. Blend until well mixed and then pour into a large mixing bowl that you can freeze safely overnight. Once frozen overnight take out the bowl carefully and scrape the top using a fork until you get a lot of fluffy Raw Organic Ice Cream that you can scoop with a spoon, you may want to freeze it again if it starts to melt or just serve right away by placing into serving bowl.

In a glass warm or hot water put in a rooibus tea bag allow it to get very dark. You can do this with room temperature water but it will take longer. Once it is very dark pour small amount into another glass then pour soda water into it until it is almost full then mix in Agave to desired sweetness about 3 to 4 tablespoons. Now you have Raw Organic Rootbeer! You can now either pour the "Raw Organic Rootbeer" into the Vanilla Raw Organic Ice Cream and serve or eat and drink separately to enjoy a new 5 Star Raw Spa Cuisine experience!

Raw Organic Ice Creams and Sorbets

Now that you know how to make Raw Organic Ice Creams without a ice cream maker machine by freezing a blended mixture with Agave and scraping the top with a fork...you can now make all sorts of different ice cream flavors and sorbets! Of course if you do happen to have a ice cream maker machine by all means use it but you don't have to have one. For different flavors try this Strawberry Ice Cream, Chocolate Ice Cream and Honey Melon Sorbet these are the best and most easy favorite flavors. You can experiment on your own of course! One of my friends even made a Beet Ice Cream it was intense but pretty good and people invent all new flavors all the time, you basically need Almond Milk, your favorite flavor ingredients, a lot of Agave to sweeten it because after you freeze it the sweetness drops a lot so you should make the mixture very sweet before freezing and you can taste it first to make sure. Remember Agave is very low sugar and low glycemic index but do use moderation in all things as well.

5 to 6 Servings or More

For Strawberry Ice Cream make the Almond Milk like on the previous page and recipe. Add about 3 cups of Strawberries with the Almond Milk and about 4 to 5 tablespoons of Agave in the Blendtec Blender, you can add more Agave to taste if desired. Blend but not too smoothly you want some chunks in there too! Pour into a freezer safe bowl, freeze overnight and scrape with a fork to make the ice cream and scoop to serve in bowls with fresh strawberries on top or other favorite berries!

For Chocolate Ice Cream make the Almond Milk like on the previous page and recipe, pour the Almond Milk into the Blendtec Blender, add 4 to 5 tablespoons of Raw Organic Carob Powder or to desired "Chocolateness", add 4 to 5 tablespoons of Agave or more to desired sweetness, you can also add a tiny bit of cinnamon and if you are into Cacao then you can add some Cacao Powder as well then blend until smooth, pour into a freezer safe bowl, freeze overnight and scrape with a fork on top until you get fluffy ice cream, scoop and serve in a bowl.

For Honey Dew Melon Sorbet, cut the honey dew in half, scoop out the seeds and plant into the ground or compost. Scoop the Honey Dew Melon and put into the Blendtec Blender, add 3 Cups of Water and about 4 to 5 tablespoons of Real Raw Agave and blend not do not blend too smoothly for a few seconds. Pour into a freezer safe bowl and freeze overnight then scrape the top with a fork with more pressure to get fluffy sorbet, scoop into a bowl and serve this refreshing heavenly sorbet is sure to delight you and put you into a 5 Star Spa state of mind!

Fruit "Sushi" Rolls

A friend of mine came up with this really interesting and unique recipe and she let me use it in my book so you can enjoy it too! It is a really cute and smart recipe made with mango as the "seaweed" and banana and raspberries as the "fruit sushi" middle. You can use my Ceramic Peeler to make the mango peels necessary to make this fun colorful recipe or "Fruishi"!
About 6 to 7 Servings or More

1 Mango
1 Banana
Raspberries
Real Raw Agave to taste

Peel the Mango using my Ceramic Peeler. Then peel long flat peelings carefully and slowly with the Ceramic Peeler or if you have really good knife skills you can use the Ceramic Knife to carefully make uniform think long "sheets" of mango to be used to make the "Fruit Sushi". I don't recommend using a Ceramic Mandolin for this because mangoes are very slippery and hard to cut so a mandolin is not safe or easy to use in this recipe. After you make enough slices and "sheets" of mango place on a plate. Peel the banana and cut small "sushi" sized pieces that will become the middle of the "Fruit Sushi" carefully wrap each banana piece with mango and you can trim it off with a Ceramic Knife but be very careful not to cut yourself! Then top with raspberries and you may drizzle some Real Raw Agave on top (optional) and serve this colorful treat! In the photo the raspberries have been crushed and mixed with Real Raw Agave before being scooped on to the banana and my friend sprinkled raw organic dried coconut on top, I don't use this ingredient often because of Gabriel Cousens MD's recommendation in The Rainbow Green Live Food Cuisine book that he wrote, I suggest you read it to get good information about different raw organic ingredients!

Open Face "Peanut Butter" Cups

This is based on a classic junk food dessert but now is transformed into the world's most healthy refreshing 5 Star Raw Spa Cuisine special recipe! Yes you CAN now enjoy "junk food" but it is now all natural and actually really good for you with maximum nutrition, vitamins, minerals and many RAWmazing benefits!
Instead of peanuts we use Raw Organic Almond Butter which has many more benefits, a lot more nutrition with better flavor and texture too!

4 Servings

1 Organic Gala Apple
Raw Organic Almond Butter
5 Tablespoons of Real Raw Agave
1/3 Cup Carob Powder
Berries and Mint for garnish (optional)

Using my 8" Ceramic Knife carefully slice even thin slices of apples and place on a serving plate.

In a mixing bowl mix the Carob Powder with Agave to make the "Chocolate Sauce". Put a spoonful of sauce on each slice of apple.

Open the jar of raw organic almond butter, almonds has the #1 amount of nutrition and benefits out of all the nuts. Put a spoonful of Almond butter on top of each "Chocolate Sauce" like in the photo and you can serve or drizzle a little more Real Raw Agave (optional) then serve. Garnish with your favorite berry and mint.

This is a great example of how 5 Star Raw Spa Cuisine is simple, elegant, fast, easy yet super nutritious and RAWmazingly RAWlicious!

58

59

Chocolate Fig Torte

Again a lot of people have requested no-nut raw organic recipes from me and here is another totally new creation of mine that I hope you will enjoy! This should only take you about 5 to 10 minutes to make and the dough will "harden" as you let it set and allow the Flax Seeds to absorb into the Banana. Here we are using the same "Doug h" from the Donut Recipe on page 50 so please go back to Page 50 and make some Raw Organic Donuts! Then use part of that "Dough" for this recipe.

About 3 to 4 Servings

Using the Donut Dough Recipe on Page 50 you can then roll small balls and flatten then put some 1/3 Cup Carob Powder mixed with 5 Tablespoons of Real Raw Agave to make the "Chocolate Sauce" in a bowl and spoon on top of the "Dough". In the photo I used special Star Cookie Cutter Shapes I found in a gourmet chef store you can use any of your favorite cookie cutter shapes of course for this recipe. I then chopped some figs which are one of my favorite Alkalizing Fruits and I put it on top to make it look and taste fancy. I also chopped half a raspberry for garnish and placed in the middle for color and flavor. But you can use your own favorite fruit toppings be creative and have fun with this recipe.

The Original Strawberry Pancakes

This is a variation of a popular raw organic pancake recipe that I have invented in 2005 that was plagiarized by another raw author which goes to show how popular my original recipe is! So I wanted to share it again since it falls under the 5 Star Raw Spa Cuisine category, what 5 Star Spa does not serve pancakes? Well now they are all natural, raw and organic which will help save our Planet in the most fun, fashionable and delicious ways possible. Now you can enjoy the true original recipe!

2 to 3 Servings

1 Cup Golden Flax Seeds
4 Tablespoons Coconut Oil in liquid form (you can use Olive Oil if you don't have Coconut Oil)
2 Tablespoons of Water

Put the golden flax seeds in the Blend-Tec blender and blend into a powder. Then pour into a bowl and mix with the rest. Use a fork and make sure to press down and mix very well until all the flax is coated and the whole mixture is really together. Split the mixture in half, form a ball with your hands and then flatten on a plate and do the same with the other half. Drizzle with Agave and enjoy. In the photo I put sliced strawberries on top with Real Raw Agave and soaked Goji Berries in the middle of each Strawberry.

Please NOTE instead of Coconut Oil you can easily use Banana which is my new recipe and technique like in the Donuts recipe on page 50. You can use that some "Dough" and new technique to make my Pancakes.

Green Tea Pistachio Ice Cream

This is a super simple recipe for a unique Asian Fusion 5 Star Raw Spa new recipe! Using organic Green Tea and Pistachios you are making fine Eco Green Cuisine! Asian Fusion recipes and cuisine is very popular in all 5 Star Spas and Resorts around the World and many are located in Asia or Southeast Asia as well.

4 to 5 Servings

Organic Green Tea loose or in a teabag
3 Cups Pure Water
2 Cups Raw Organic Pistachios shelled
5 to 6 Tablespoons of Real Raw Agave to taste

You can soak the Green Tea in room temperature or warm water and let soak to desired level of Tea flavor. Then pour into the Blendtec Blender.

In the Blendtec Blender (you can get at a great discount from my website for only $350 tax/shipping/handling included, this is the Best Blender in the World that is why I recommend and suggest it so much!) add all the ingredients and blend until smooth.

Pour into a freezer safe bowl and freeze until solid and hard overnight. The next day carefully take out of the freezer and scrape with a fork with added pressure look at photo to the right. When you scrape enough Ice Cream use a spoon or ice cream scooper to make scoops and serve. You can drizzle some Real Raw Agave mixed with some Raw Organic Carob Powder to make a "Chocolate Sauce" and drizzle on top, add your favorite berries. The Green Tea has fantastic Anti-oxidants and benefits. Serve on a warm hot day and enjoy!

Candied Apples

People ask me for fun Holiday Raw Organic Recipes all the time so I always will come up with something when people request it from me because I am here to make people happy and healthy! Also many people will spend the Holidays at 5 Star Spas and Resorts to relax and to connect with nature or to just enjoy it in a different setting. This is a super fun recipe that kids and adults both love. And it only takes about 2 minutes for each Candied Apple!

3 to 4 Servings

3 to 4 Organic Gala Apples
Raw Organic Walnuts, Almonds, Pecans
7 Tablespoons of Real Raw Agave
1 Cup of Raw Organic Carob Powder
Drink Mixing Sticks or Chopsticks for the Apple

Wash the Apples and I find Gala to work best but use your favorite type of Apple. Dry the Apples and push a mixing stick or chopstick into the top of the Apple.

In a large mixing bowl combine the Carob Powder with the Real Raw Agave until you get the desired consistency, less Agave for a thicker "Chocolate Sauce" and more for a liquid softer sauce. After mixing by hand using a fork, use a spoon to coat the apples then chop the nuts and sprinkle around the sauce and serve. Kids and adults love this fun easy recipe and it is so delicious while being low sugar. Enjoy the Holidays and share the gift of love, laughter and health with your friends, family then the World!

67

Cookie Dough

You may not find this at a 5 Star Spa but sometimes they have treats to keep their guests happy. Now they can with this very gourmet version of a junk food favorite. This recipe can be made in a variety of ways.

4 to 5 Servings

1 Jar of Raw Organic Sprouted Macadamia Nut Butter or regular Macadamia Nut Butter (not mixed with Cashew)
Or
1 Jar of Raw Organic Tahini
3 to 4 Tablespoons of Real Raw Agave
Sundried Mulberry
Cacao Nibs

If you can find the Sprouted Macadamia Nut Butter than that works the best for this recipe the next best is regular Macadamia Nut Butter and then the 3rd Alternative is Raw Organic Tahini. If you can find the Sprouted Macadamia Nut Butter then simply spoon some from the jar and stir in some Cacao Nibs and Sundried Mulberry and serve, you can drizzle Real Raw Agave (optional) to sweeten it a little.

If you can't find the sprouted version then use the regular Raw Organic Macadamia Nut Butter but you may have to freeze it to make it harden and it may not stay hard or solid for long, especially if you live I a hot or warm climate, in that case use the next version!

Open a jar of Raw Organic Tahini and scoop with a spoon into a mixing bowl and stir in the Agave, Cacao Nibs and Sundried Mulberry, form into "Cookie Dough" balls and serve! You can put it on top of Raw Organic Ice Cream, eat it as is or serve next to your fruit smoothie. Macadamia Nut Butter and Tahini are very healthy and nutritious so once again a total favorite junk food recipe is now transformed into the most healthy recipe in the World!

69

Raw Cola, RAW Dew, RAW Up, RAW Ginger Ale

I will admit it when I was little I used to love to drink sodas and colas but later on wow did I regret that! I also wondered why anyone would make anything so toxic and bad for you and sell it all around the World? But now there is a safe, low sugar and healthy Raw Organic Version of course!

1 to 2 Servings

Rooibus Tea or regular dark tea
Green Tea organic of course
Fresh Ginger
Club Soda Water
Lime or Lemon

This recipe is very simple really. Ok for the **RAW Cola** put the Rooibus tea bag or dark tea in water or warm water and allow to soak until desired color and flavor. Stir in with a spoon or fork Real Raw Agave to desired sweetness then add Club Soda Water and ice cubes stir again and enjoy!

RAW Dew: is Organic Green Tea in water, Real Raw Agave, Club Soda Water mix and stir well with a spoon or fork and add ice cubes.

RAW Up: Real Raw Agave, Club Soda Water, squeeze of Lime or Lemon, stir by hand and add ice and stir some more then serve with slice of lime or lemon.

RAW Ginger Ale: Real Raw Agave, Grated fresh Ginger, Club Soda Water, stir by hand with spoon or fork, add ice stir some more and enjoy!

71

72

Cosmic Green Smoothie

Every 5 Star Spa serves a Green Smoothie which is very healthy, refreshing, alkalizing and more! I have one almost every morning and I know many people who enjoy them as a healthy fast breakfast on the go. I have made different kinds but I found this recipe to be the most RAWmazing, after I drank it I felt instantly at ONE with the entire Universe and I actually felt it working through my body in a healthy way. It is so healthy that WOW you have to experience this for yourself!

2 Servings

~ Dandelion Greens(bitter and detox super green, will help rejuvenate your kidney and liver which filters your blood and body, buy from a health food store most Whole Foods Markets have it).
~ Dino Kale (Super green some people usually do not eat but perfect in a green smoothie)
~ 1 Lime (activate enzymes and energy)
~ ½ Pineapple (increases digestion, flavor, optional but good!)
~ Some Goji Berry (Happy!)
~ A few spoonfuls Coconut oil (just a little for anti-aging effects)
~ 1 Avocado (makes it creamy and benefits too! Optional)
~ 1 Banana (sweetness and flavor to balance out all the bitter greens, some people don't do bananas I love 'em)
~ 1 Orange (flavor and vitamin C)
~ Touch of Real Raw Agave (energy and sweet)
~ 1 Kombucha (anti radiation, anti-emf, anti-aging)
~ Cayenne Pepper (increases digestion and circulation)
~ Spicy hot pepper (increases digestion and circulation)
~ Some Broccoli Sprouts (bitter which is detox I read if you eat the sprouts it is better and more nutritious than eating the broccoli florets)
2 Cups of water adjust to desired thickness of smoothie

Put all the above ingredients in the Blendtec Blender, blend until smooth and enjoy and feel the bliss!

Thank you for joining in the 5 Star Raw Spa Cuisine with Chef Bryan Au adventure I hope you enjoyed each and every recipe as I have put all of my heart and soul into each page and I want to share the best of what I have to offer with your, your loved ones and the World.

My true healing intentions is to add more health, harmony, love, peace and joy to our Planet. It is a big world to save and a portion of proceeds goes to planting new trees and every purchase you make from my website or any of my products actually will help fund a new planting of a tree and other eco green or humanitarian non profit organizations around the World.

Raw Organic Saving The Planet is about empowering you to save the Earth in the most fun, fashionable and delicious ways possible!

Now I have listed what I believe to be the best products, the highest quality and at the best most affordable prices for you to enjoy. Many people also ask me where they can get certain Ingredients as they are not always readily available in their location, city or town so I have listed all the contact information, stores, websites as I can and have also included a list of where you can buy my products as well. One of my future plans is to open a National Raw Organic Food/Bookstore/Spa Franchise where people can come to enjoy my special Raw Organic Cuisine, Food, Snacks, Eco Bamboo Organic Cotton Fashions, Books, DVDs, Ceramic Knives, Blendtec Blenders and much more. People can come enjoy the best food, snacks, smoothies, books and do some Yoga, take some classes and much more so if you are interested in supporting, owning your own future possible franchise or for more investment information or if you have any questions, ideas or suggestions please e-mail me directly at RawBryan@hotmail.com

From top left to right: New Cute Eco Bamboo Organic T-shirt fashion line now you can wear Raw Organic Clothing! Two scenes from my new National Raw Organic TV Show which will air Nationwide on TV and I teach 4 of my Raw Organic Recipes from my first Edition book and 2nd Edition Book: RAW IN TEN MINUTES and RAW FOOD IN TEN MINUTES. The first Edition has a very interesting story that I am writing my Autobiography on because people want to know how I became a Raw Organic Chef and how I self published my book, did all my own marketing, Website, networking and built my Raw Organic Career to success in just 3 short years after coming out with my self published 1st Edition book. It is a very amazing and entertaining new book that will teach you everything I learned, all my successful techniques, each step of the way. All my stories, jokes, advice, the actual websites I used to find investors, supporters, fans and to increase sales and much more I will reveal EVERYTHING in my all new Autobiography titled: Bryan Au how I got into the RAW! The Real RAW Story! You will learn EVERYTHING like how to become a successful Raw Organic Chef, what it really takes to succeed in the publishing business but you can apply ALL of my techniques to ANY BUSINESS and to make any industry, business, online store succeed and become a National Success. You can learn it all from my new Autobiography coming out soon. Next is the Blendtec Blender I can honestly say that it allowed me to tap into all the creativity that I needed to invent totally new never before seen Raw Organic Recipes. It takes true professional equipment to bring out all your hidden gifts, talents and abilities that is one of many "secrets" that I reveal that as a Chef you have to have the best kitchen equipment possible and I have the BEST Prices on it all on my website online store for only $350 including tax/shipping/handling you can get your own high tech Blendtec Blender the "Rolls Royce" of Blenders and the best in the World. Next is my friend and one of my models Casey she is a Celebrity in Hollywood and a actress that volunteered to model some of my Eco Bamboo Organic Fashions for Men and Women which will be available nationwide soon and is on my website currently: http://www.RawInTen.com . Next is the totally new Good4U Dehydrator this is a very innovative pretty design that is functional and the best Dehydrator on the market at the best price only $150 for the 10 tray on my website, notice you can see through the innovative design and the motor is very quiet and efficient. None of my recipes has Dehydrating in them in any of my books but I am actually almost done with my special new Raw Organic Dehydrating book just for the new Good4U Dehydrator! All the recipes are still under 10 Minutes to make and then so many hours in the Dehydrator some totally new ones I created are hot fluffy pancakes that looks and taste just like the cooked ones but this is healthier and sprouted, I also have a new Upside Down Pineapple Cake and so many more totally new Dehydrated Raw Organic Recipe book coming out soon! I will add more photos and information in the next few pages, enjoy!

The above is Sherry Modeling the new Eco Bamboo Organic Cotton fashion line designed by me, soon to be in all the stores nationwide. They are infused with messages of Peace, Raw Organic Lifestyle and Health in fun fashionable way. There is also my Ceramic Knife that also allowed me to make precision cuts to invent totally new raw organic recipes, it also keeps food pure, fresher longer and really saves you money, people love my price, quality and value of all my Ceramic Knives and Ceramic Peelers. Below is another Peace Slogan because "Raw is War spelled backwards because now we are waging Peace!"-Bryan Au available as a poster or free download soon on my website: http://www.RawInTen.com I'm always available to teach classes and do lectures.

This is the Ultimate Super Foods Brand of Real Raw Organic Agave this is the only Agave I will use and recommend in all my raw organic food and sales because it literally is the best quality, is really raw, at the best price is better than using dates because is low sugar and you can order it directly from me on my website online store: **http://www.RawInTen.com**

The Spouted Ground Flax Seeds product to the left is what I used in all my photos and I like to recommend this Flax Seed brand because they did a wonderful job in sprouting it and then grounding it for the perfect consistency, it is so easy and fun to use I recommend getting this instead of making a big mess in the kitchen you can just pour it out and it is still very fresh full of amino acids and a special process they used so that is healthy naturally. It will be available on my website soon as well.

This is the World's Only 8" Ceramic Knife in the World and is my favorite. It literally stays super sharp for 2 years without having to sharp it each time like dull metal knives that wear out, it will never rust, is very pure and keeps food fresher longer so saves a lot of money. I use this 8" Ceramic Knife the most and is the one I would get if I had to only use one knife.

100% RAW ORGANIC
CUISINE IN TEN
MINUTES DVD

How to make the best
Raw Organic Meals,
Desserts, Snacks all
in just 10 Minutes!

Bryan Au

Upper Left: more of my Eco Bamboo Organic Cotton Denim fashions and jeans available soon! Middle: Cover of my popular instructional RAW FOOD DVDs that is expanding to more in the popular series of DVDs. And me on the set of my National Raw Organic Food TV Show this is a World's First on National TV so is making history and I hope to benefit the entire Raw Organic Food Community and Unite this Industry and make it #1, Mainstream, the next Major Food Trend, Major Diet and Lifestyle!

I also want to recommend signing up and using Elements For Life Brand of Goji Berries and other raw organic ingredients that you may be looking for or enjoy they have the best and you can start a great home based raw organic business as many people would like to promote health, well being and find different sources of income and wealth, please join under my special link here:

https://www.noblelifeelements.com/rawbryan

Thank you again and if you have any questions you would like to ask me, I am always available to do media interviews, teach classes, do presentations and lectures, please e-mail me at:

RawBryan@hotmail.com

I would like to wish you the best in health, wealth, joy, happiness, spirit, strength, abundance and peace forever and RAWays,

Raw Organic Chef Bryan Au

http://www.RawInTen.com

The meaning behind the RAW STAR LOGO is that when you are into Raw Organic Food and Lifestyle it is the most Eco Green Cuisine possible so you are literally a RAW STAR and a Super Hero as you are saving and protecting your health, community, the environment and the entire World! It is a big planet to save but I am very honored to help empower everyone in the most fun, fashionable and delicious ways possible! So I hope you can continue to enjoy and support my products so we can all be more RAW ORGANIC SAVING THE PLANET !

Notes

Notes

Notes

Notes

Notes

Notes

Notes

Notes

Notes

Notes

Notes

Notes

Notes

2251902

Made in the USA